Have you picked your pumpkin?

1

A pumpkin seed
is tucked into
sun-warmed earth.
Spring rains soften
its tough coat.

A root reaches
for nutrients.
A sprout reaches
for light.

Soon jagged leaves
rise from twisty
vines wandering in
all directions.

Bees visit golden blossoms, spreading pollen from flower to flower.

Here and there, tiny green knobs replace wilted flowers.

The knobs change color and slowly swell, growing heavier by the day.

Cooler nights arrive. Vines shrivel.

Left behind are
pumpkins, pumpkins,
pumpkins!

Pumpkins are a type of squash.

They can be green, red, tan, yellow, white, or even blue.

The pumpkins we know best are bright orange.

There are **tall** pumpkins. SHORT pumpkins.

Smooth or bumpy pumpkins.

Wee ones, only inches wide, or GIANTS you can sit inside.

Thump-thump-thump.

A pumpkin sounds hollow, but inside is stringy wet pulp and oodles of slippery white seeds.

Seeds might be saved to grow next year's pumpkins or dried for a crunchy snack.

Pumpkin pulp smells sharp and tangy, but can be made into delicious breads, desserts, and soups.

Sugar pumpkins go into the spicy pies we bring to our Thanksgiving tables.

The End.

Unless ... was there something else pumpkins might be used for?

Oh, yes.

Jack-'o-lanterns!

Will you give yours a funny face or a creepy one to send shivers up your back?

Will it be the head of a straw-filled scarecrow?

Will your Jack-'o-lantern decorate your kitchen table among striped gourds and sunset-colored leaves?

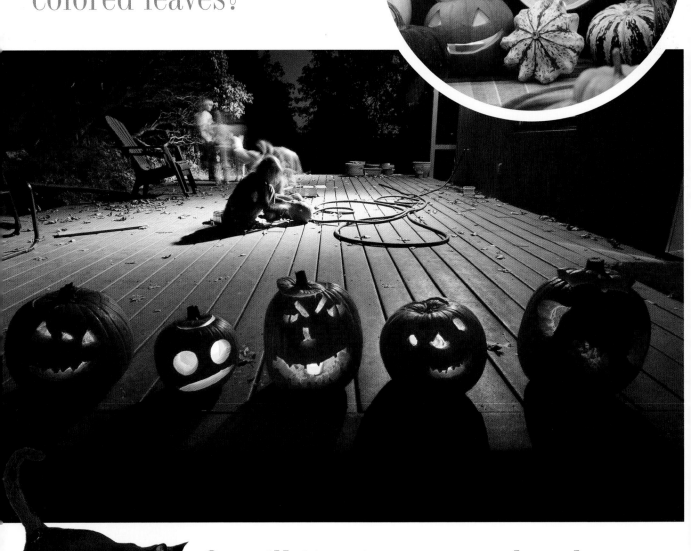

Or will it set your porch aglow on a spooky Halloween night, lighting the way for a curious cat?

Unused pumpkins
are fed to farm
animals or left in the
field to nourish the
precious soil...

...awaiting spring under a wintry blanket.